Reflections of an HR Caveman

Going Back to the Basics

I0474153

Gary Montavon

outskirtspress
DENVER, COLORADO

Outskirts Press, Inc.
http://www.outskirtspress.com

ISBN: 978-1-4787-7446-4

Outskirts Press and the "OP" logo are trademarks belonging to Outskirts Press, Inc.

PRINTED IN THE UNITED STATES OF AMERICA

This book is dedicated to my wife, Barbara, our children, Leigh and Brian and to our lovely granddaughter, Tillie.

Preface

A couple of years ago, I started blogging to call attention to positive employee relations practices, to serve as a primer for rising Human Resources professionals and, optimistically, to reach the hundreds of thousands of small businesses who cannot afford a dedicated Human Resources person. It was my objective that my blog would be viewed as a simple and straightforward presentation of useful and practical information. I had retired a year earlier and there were many things in our Human Resources world I felt strongly about and wanted to address.

Having fallen somewhat short on reaching each and every one of those hundreds of thousands of small businesses with my blogs, I decided to change direction. The result is this book. With it, I intend to tie my previous postings together and more.

I wrote this book because I still care. I care about how employees are treated by companies. I care about companies being profitable and successful. I care about Human Resources, my chosen profession. I want HR professionals, old and new, to be reminded of what constitutes the foundation of our Human Resources agenda. I cover basic principles and philosophies that have withstood the test of time and will serve you well in any industry and in any economic environment, anywhere in the world.

I wrote this book at this particular time because we are in a business climate of relative calm, lower unemployment and increasing pressure to find and keep good employees who now have choices and opportunities to go elsewhere. If ever there was a time to revisit the Human Resources agenda, it is now.

I retired after working over 36 years in Human Resources at the plant, division, group and corporate level. I have had the good fortune of sitting in all of the seats. I have had my "seat at the table." I have worked domestically and internationally.

It is not that I disagree with the direction Human Resources seems to be taking today as everyone is working hard to keep up in an ever-changing and ever-evolving work world. It is the fact that, in keeping up, I believe many Human Resources professionals have strayed from the basics, those very tenets and principles that made us a significant and successful discipline in the first place.

I chose the title *Reflections of an HR Caveman* to make a couple of points. The first is to demonstrate to the reader that I have "been there and done that." Secondly, and more importantly, to reflect on basic principles and practices that will serve as the foundation and building blocks for any Human Resources function. I reference several "old" articles and statistics throughout the book. It is not that I was unable to find current day articles and statistics to make my points. It is to show that even though time marches on, many of the principles, practices and solutions effectively used by companies years ago are still applicable today.

I am not dismissing current day HR challenges, issues and opportunities. I am as concerned with important issues like gender discrimination, workplace bullying, new immigration policy, quickie election rule changes and talent analytics as the next person, but my focus will be on taking you back to the basics, those principles that never change. The caveman in me knows that if you get the basics right, most everything else will take care of itself.

In order to give you an idea what kind of an HR leader your author was I start this book with some quotes, tips and insights that were meaningful and useful to me through the years. Chapter 1 speaks to our HR agenda and why companies should have a Human Resources function. Chapter 2 describes many areas Human Resources can and should be leading and facilitating in order to help their company achieve "employer of choice" status. Chapter 3 covers "what's in it for employees" and describes several different actions a company can take to prove they value their employees as their greatest assets. Chapter 4 is a quick discussion on HR's responsibility to be the company's ethics conscience and chief steward. Chapters 5 and 6 focus on communications as the foundation of employee engagement through open, transparent and two-way communication. Chapters 7 and 8 describe tools every HR professional should consider having in their toolbox, as well as a brief discussion of some key and fundamental practices, policies and procedures. In Chapter 9, I close with some reflections from my years in Human Resources and what I feel it will take for Human Resources functions everywhere to be successful in the years to come.

My intended audience has not changed. I am still hopeful this book will be useful to rising HR Professionals and will also resonate with smaller business concerns that do not have the size and scope to warrant a dedicated HR resource. This book can also serve as a refresher for HR professionals in larger organizations. Enjoy!

HR Quotes, Tips and Truisms

Have you ever caught yourself saying to a co-worker, "You can't make this stuff up. I should write a book someday." Well, I did.

The following Human Resources-related quotes, tips and truisms I came across throughout my career are intended to give you a glimpse of what resonates with me and how I see and reflect on Human Resources and situations in the workplace.

- We all know someone in the workplace who tends to be left out of activities because they are different. Step outside of your comfort zone today and reach out to someone who is NOT like you. Have an inclusive day!

- *"Safety is something that happens between your ears, not something you hold in your hands"* - John Dean "Jeff" Cooper

- Conducting staff meetings on a monthly basis can be difficult at times but your employees really do want and need to know what is going on.

- Find a success to celebrate and generate some excitement in the workplace this week.

- I once worked for a division of a company that was so proud of the turkeys they distributed at Thanksgiving that they decided to ask their employees how they felt about them on their annual employee opinion survey. One employee responded, "Turkey? I thought it was a chicken!"

- You don't have to like the people you work with in order to do a good job but it sure is a heck of a lot more fun when you do.

- *"If you pick the right people and give them the opportunity to spread their wings and put compensation as a carrier behind it, you almost don't have to manage them"* - Jack Welch

- Do something today that makes your employees feel like they really are your greatest asset.

- Open houses can be a big hit with your employees and their families. Children like to see where their parents go and know what they do when they leave the house each day.

- There is no need to wait until April each year. If you are fortunate enough to have one, thank your administrative assistant today for all of the support s/he gives you.

- *"Find a job you like and you add five days to every week"* - H. Jackson Brown

- Write a personal note to someone today recognizing an achivement or thanking them for a special contribution. It feels good, doesn't it?

- Companies are in business to make money, not to make employees happy. But, it sure is great when you can find one that can do both.

- Seek out a recently hired employee today and ask him/her how they are getting acclimated and if they need anything from you.

- Everyone wants to be spoken to by name. Don't you?

- Never confide in one employee about another employee. You may think they will be pleased you are taking them into confidence but, in reality, you are just scaring them. They will quickly come to the realization that if you are willing to talk to them about another employee, you will do the same to them.

- Check your list of upcoming work anniversary milestones. Find someone on the list, leave your office and personally thank that employee for their service.

- Plan a community help project this week. Your employees will volunteer to help you with it. The break from the routine will be good for them and your community will benefit.

- Promise yourself, "I will not send an email to the person in the office next to me today."

- Encourage a manager to give recognition to one of his/her employees today.

- Tell your boss one thing s/he really needs to know but everyone is afraid to tell her/him. It will help the organization and you will be seen in a different light.

- If you do not understand how your business works or

how your product is made, don't be embarrassed or shy. Ask someone to explain it to you. They will enjoy telling you and you will learn something and become more valuable to your organization.

Contents

Preface i
HR Quotes, Tips and Truisms v

1: **Why Are We Here?** 1
Thank You, Joseph Coates! 2
Take Your Seat At The Table! 3
My Ideal HR Professional 3
HR Generalist or HR Specialist? 5

2: **Becoming an Employer of Choice** 7
Who Wants To Be An Employer Of Choice? 8
It Still Isn't Rocket Science! 9

3: **Showing You Care** 12
HR And The 1-800 Number 12
Safety First. Really! 13
Simplifying Wellness - Pack Your Shoes 15
Here I Am. Does Anybody See Me? 18
Performance Appraisal -
Who Says It Has To Be Complicated? 19
Organization Reviews Are Not Just For The Big Dogs ...23
Do We Do What We Say We Do? 24

4: Ethics 27
　　Business Ethics - Your Employees Are Watching You! 27

5: Communications 29
　　Effective Communications - Really!...........................29
　　Annual State-of-the-Business Address.......................31
　　Monthly Site Meetings...31
　　Weekly Staff And Supervisor Meetings 32
　　Weekly Toolbox Meetings...32
　　Employee Opinion Survey..33
　　Employee Opinion Surveys:
　　The Granddaddy Of Them All!...................................33
　　Your Employees Are Talking To You. Are You Listening?....36

6: Employee Engagement 40
　　Why Are We Still Talking About Employee Engagement?..40

7: Technology, Tools, Goals and Analytics 43
　　What's In Your Toolbox?...43
　　The Data Will Set You Free! 46
　　HR Goal Setting. Getting Started...............................46

8: Practices, Policies and Procedures 49
　　Who Gets To Stay? 49
　　Hire Slowly, Fire Quickly 50
　　Employee Retention - Keeping The Good Ones............52
　　Senior Management Retention Checklist 52
　　Why Do You Stay? 55
　　Temporary Employees - The Good, The Bad, The Ugly! . 56
　　Welcome To Management! Acclimating New Managers .. 63
　　Some Thoughts On Leadership 65
　　Automatic Wage Progression 67

9: Conclusion...**71**

Acknowledgements..73

1

Why Are We Here?

Who needs HR? My simple answer, "Anyone operating a business who has employees working for them." A better question might be, "Who needs a dedicated HR person?" While this question has been debated through the years, I believe it becomes important to have a dedicated resource once you reach 100 employees. Regardless of company size, the agenda is the same. It just becomes a matter of who leads and facilitates the agenda and who does the work.

The Human Resources agenda is to attract, retain and develop employees. It looks simple when you put it into writing but we all know there are a countless number of activities that must take place in order to execute that agenda. Throughout my career, there was an ending to the agenda statement that read, "in a non-union environment." I will not elaborate on that point in this book other than to say it has always been my preference to work in companies who worked hard to preserve their right to work directly with their employees without the interference of a third party.

REFLECTIONS OF AN HR CAVEMAN

The following are my thoughts on the need for motivating HR professionals to be as effective as they can be, taking their seat at the table, what an ideal HR professional looks like and some discussion on choosing to become an HR specialist or an HR generalist.

Thank You, Joseph Coates!

I had the good fortune of working with many wonderful HR professionals throughout my career. I never felt the need to seek out motivational products or programs to light a fire under anyone. Actually, I am not sure I would have known where to look if I did. Then, one day, I came across a statement by a Washington Futurist by the name of Joseph Coates. He said, "HR professionals are stuck in being second-tier and being executors of decisions that other people make, rather than being on equal footing in the strategic planning of the organization. There is nothing on the horizon to indicate any change to this set up."

To this day, this statement offends me to the core. How about you? Since coming across it, I cannot begin to tell you how many times I have used this quote in meetings with HR professionals; ones who worked for me as well as many who didn't. If you ever feel the need to motivate HR staff to take pride in the importance of their chosen profession and to take full responsibility for the quality of the work they do, I believe this is your ticket. Thank you, Joseph Coates! You have given a gift that keeps on giving.

Take Your Seat At The Table!

After the first 25 years or so of my career, I began to feel when it came to most anything having to do with Human Resources I had "been there, done that." While I truly had traveled to many places and truly had done many things, if I had it to do all over again, there is clearly one area I would have approached differently. I would have worked harder at staying abreast of what was happening in our Human Resources universe. That being said, there are exceptions to every rule, even the rule I just made up about staying abreast of what is happening in HR. My exception centers around paying any attention whatsoever to the countless number of articles that have been written through the years about Human Resources leaders and their "seat at the table." I grow weary with this HR coming out, "You have finally arrived as a real function," angle.

My view on these articles and my advice to you on this matter is far different from what is generally written. If you are the Human Resources leader at your corporation, group, division, plant, office or store, "Take your seat at the table!" If someone asks you to leave because they don't feel you belong, I strongly recommend you do so and then, quickly, initiate your search for a real Human Resources position. The same goes for working in any organization where you, as the HR leader, are asked to report to anyone other than the CEO or top management individual in that business.

My Ideal HR Professional

I have read the articles. I have seen the lists. I understand if you ask 20 different people you will get 20 different answers. Still, for me, the ideal HR professional looks a lot like the following. I tried to boil my list down to a "Top 10" but I failed. Sorry!

My ideal HR professional:

- is smart but also has a lot of common sense.

- has a burning intellectual curiosity to learn more, to keep on asking why and how.

- has a natural ability and desire to engage people.

- exudes an aura of approachability that shouts "welcome" to employees.

- enjoys the challenge of solving difficult employee relations problems.

- has a general disdain for the administrative requirements of the position but an ability to manage the minutia.

- is a creative thinker who refuses to ever believe one size fits all.

- is a born collaborator and is inclusive by nature.

- has general business know-how and is interested in understanding how the company's product or service works.

- thinks globally.

- has the confidence and fortitude to stand by his/her convictions.

- is emotionally balanced and measured.

- prefers spending time with employees in the workplace to hiding away in his/her office.

- has integrity.

I don't know about you, but I would love to work with a staff of HR professionals with these characteristics.

HR Generalist or HR Specialist?

So, you're interested in pursuing a career in Human Resources and you can't decide whether to follow a generalist or specialist path. The good news is there are no wrong answers here. I know many very successful and professionally fulfilled HR generalists and I know just as many very successful and professionally fulfilled HR specialists. While having a definitive plan is always a good approach, the outcome will generally be dictated by time, place and opportunity, not your plan.

I spent an entire career harping on the merits of being a generalist to anyone who would listen. I couldn't understand why anyone would want to spend their time doing the same thing day in and day out. While I am still inclined to feel this way, it's funny how careers play out. I knew I wanted a career in Human Resources. I thought I wanted to be a generalist and to have a hand in everything from attracting to retaining to developing employees.

As I retrace my steps and look back at how things unfolded, I quickly come to realize I spent many of my working years doing specialist HR work. My first professional position was as a labor relations specialist. It was an eye opener. I learned early on I wanted to work in companies who worked hard at operating union-free and who valued dealing directly with their employees and not through a third party. Next, I spent several years as an employee opinion survey specialist. To this day, I can think of no better communications platform with employees than a well-executed employee opinion survey. I also had the opportunity to perform specialist work with wage and salary proposals and executive compensation. I have always viewed my time in compensation as being a "great place to be from." Spend some time working in compensation and, as you progress through the organization, you will never have to accept the answer, "We don't do that here."

My point? Human Resources, unlike many professions, allows for considerable choice. That's a good thing. Find a good company. Try it all. Let things unfold. If you find a specialty area you love, go for it. If not, you will find when all is said and done, you have become a very well-rounded generalist.

2

Becoming an Employer of Choice

Becoming an employer of choice is a lofty aspiration. Every company I have ever worked in has wanted to be one, but I have worked in very few where we have stayed focused on the prize and actually achieved it. Becoming an employer of choice is hard work and everybody from the CEO to the person you hire tomorrow must be actively involved and on board. Leaders need to lead and inspire. Employees need to know exactly what is expected of them. Managers need to make themselves available to listen, coach and counsel and then stay out of their employees' way and empower them to perform.

It isn't rocket science but it still is hard work; very hard work. But, if you are willing to exert the time and energy and you get it right, you will be rewarded with loyalty and your employees will give you their very best efforts.

Who Wants To Be An Employer Of Choice?

I think the answer to this is easy. We all do. Achieving employer of choice status is a much more difficult proposition. I have wrestled a bit with whether the following are attributes or philosophies but, in the end, I don't think it really matters. What I do know is that through time these same characteristics are almost always present in the most successful operations.

1. Safety first! Though it was #2 in Abraham Maslow's hierarchy of needs, I won't be too critical here. He did have it right up there after our biological and physiological needs for air, food, drink, shelter, warmth, intimacy and sleep.

2. Effective two-way communication is understood as being essential.

3. Organization planning and employee development are seen as keys to survival.

4. The Human Resources staff is seen as being strong employee advocates while, at the same time, having the ability to balance the needs of the business.

5. Training, many say "learning" these days, is aligned with business needs and is ongoing.

6. There is an emphasis on training first-line supervisors (and group leaders, if they are present in the organization).

7. Diversity is seen as a positive attribute and is embraced.

8. Employee recognition programs are critical.

9. Salary and benefit programs are competitive but are also managed.

10. Floor time, floor time, floor time. In days gone by, this would have been referred to as "management-by-walking-around."

11. A strong business ethics program is in place and is understood by all.

12. There is a strong preference for operating union-free.

13. Hire slowly, fire quickly.

I touch on each of these characteristics within this book. I have enjoyed working in companies where these attributes and philosophies were present. Wouldn't you?

It Still Isn't Rocket Science!

I re-read an article the other day about the 100 best companies to work for in America. It wasn't until I finished the article that I realized it was written in 1984. Yep, it was written over 30 years ago. You may have seen articles and lists like these through the years. This particular one went on to say that people are proud to work for companies that treat them well and it's this feeling more than any other that sets them apart. What a novel concept!

I cannot begin to recall the names of those 100 special companies in 1984, but I do remember scribbling down the characteristics they all seemed to have in common. These are timeless qualities and characteristics. They were true over 30 years ago. They are true today. They will be true 30 years from now.

1. Good pay and competitive benefits.

2. Make employees feel like they part of the team.

3. Encourage open communications.

4. Promote from within wherever possible.

5. Stress quality. It gives employees pride in the products and services they are providing.

6. Allow employees to share in the profits and the success of the company.

7. Reduce distinctions of rank between top management and those in lower level positions.

8. Devote attention and resources to creating a pleasant workplace.

9. Help employees by matching the funds they save.

10. Minimize layoffs.

11. Care enough about the health of employees to provide physical fitness centers and regular health programs.

12. Expand the skills of employees through training programs.

13. Lead ethically and with integrity.

It bears repeating that these characteristics of a good company were sourced from a 30-year-old article. The list is not so different from the employer of choice list, is it? I would certainly think these 100 companies were employers of choice in their day, wouldn't you?

When all is said and done, I believe it's the journey toward employer of choice status that sets companies apart. I am not smart enough to look in on different companies and say who has achieved it and who hasn't but I am able to quickly recognize the efforts of companies who are aspiring to do right by their employees. When your employees begin to want the same things for your business you do you will be well on your way. Their reward will be the peace of mind that they are working in a company who cares about them as an individual. Your reward will be retention and employee's best efforts

3

Showing You Care

Maybe I should have changed the title of this chapter to, Proving You Care. It's easy to develop recruiting materials and expound on all of the things your company is going to do for employees once they are on board. It's another thing to actually fulfill those recruiting material promises. Let me expand a bit on what "things" I am referring to. It starts with satisfying the basic needs of safety and protection and then includes such "things" as listening to, encouraging, coaching, developing and challenging employees to reach their potential and to excel.

The following topics touch on a few of the approaches companies can adopt to show (prove) they care about their employees.

HR And The 1-800 Number

In the interest of keeping this clean, I will refer to this as the "1-800 we don't care about you as an individual" number. I understand and appreciate the need for speed, efficiency and real-time this and that in the world we live in today but, be careful. There has to be a balanced approach here. Not all of your employees are capable and comfortable in that world. For a variety of reasons, many of your employees are not DIYers. You run the risk of alienating these employees if the only message they are receiving from Human Resources is, "I don't have time for you. It's online. Figure it out."

I would suggest working with employees who come to you on matters like these is as important a responsibility of Human Resources as anything you do. I would never wish a union organizing campaign on anybody, but who do you think your employees are going to turn to in an organization where there are limited HR touches and where the 1-800 number is their "primary" channel of communication?

Safety First. Really!

According to the Bureau of Labor Statistics, the number of fatal occupational injuries in the U.S. fell 5% in 2013. The national fatality rate for non-farm workers fell from 3.4 deaths per 100,000 workers in 2012 to 3.2 deaths per 100,000 workers in 2013. While we should all be pleased with any amount of improvement in this area, hold your applause. Do the math. A 3.2 deaths per 100,000 rate on total U.S. non-farm employment in the neighborhood of 157 million workers means over 5,000 of our fathers, mothers, husbands, wives, partners, brothers, sisters, sons, daughters, friends and co-workers went to work in 2013 and never returned home.

Safety has to become top of mind in all companies. The leaders of companies have a responsibility and obligation to do everything within their means to ensure employees leave their organizations at the end of every working day in the same condition in which they arrived. Employees have a right to work in companies where they will be safe, where they are encouraged to bring safety concerns and issues to the attention of management knowing they will be fully considered.

I had the pleasure of working with a senior executive who willingly took the time from an extremely busy schedule to visit any location within the corporation at any time to celebrate major safety achievements and milestones. The theme of his message to employees was always the same. While many things will happen in a business over the course of an employee's career that are easily forgotten, the one thing employees will always remember is where they were and what they were doing on the day when they first heard about a lost time accident at their facility or, God forbid, the death of a co-worker. Safety is your legacy. It needs to be treated with the care and respect it deserves.

Some safety thoughts and considerations:

1. No one gets to delegate the responsibility for safety to one individual or one department. Safety is everyone's responsibility.

2. Working in a safe environment is every employee's right.

3. Safety suggestion programs are a win-win. Employees will bring you issues you may otherwise be unaware of and they will feel good about the fact you are interested in their safety and are asking them for their input.

4. Celebrate your safety successes. Now that I am retired,

my wife and I travel a lot. As we drive from place to place and city to city, I always point out the banners I see flying high and the big signs on the sides of facilities proclaiming to all the number of hours their business has gone without a lost time accident. I think they are great, and I am certain the employees in those businesses do, too.

5. Safety incentive programs are a good thing but they should come with a warning label that says, "Beware a culture of too many safety incentive programs. You may be encouraging non-reporting."

6. Companies with detailed management systems for safety and environmental protection are likely to be much more successful because they tend to do things right the first time, minimizing operational upsets, regulatory intervention and the costs of non-compliance.

Simplifying Wellness - Pack Your Shoes
I love the focus that has been placed on wellness programs over the last several years. Motive doesn't matter. Employee wellness is positive for everyone. Everybody wins. Employees feel better. Performance goes up. Productivity improves. Health insurance costs go down. So, why hasn't everyone jumped on this bandwagon? I recently read that 50% of companies with over 50 employees have some form of a wellness program. Am I supposed to be impressed? What about the other 50%? What about the hundreds of thousands of companies with fewer than 50 employees?

Anyone and everyone can have a wellness program. If ever

there was a place for the well-worn phrase, "this isn't rocket science," it's here. I had a personal wellness program throughout my entire working career. I called it, "pack your shoes." I ran in every city and in every country in which I ever worked. I ran with someone from the location I was visiting every chance I got. My "pack your shoes" wellness program helped me physically, emotionally and psychologically. It kept me sane. Over 30,000 documented running miles later, I would highly recommend it.

OK, so maybe my wellness program isn't for everybody. There is still no excuse for not starting some form of a program personally or in your company immediately. Sure, there are issues to be worked through here and there but the pros far outweigh the cons.

Some pros: (NOTE: There is absolutely no science behind these. They are personal observations.)

1. Employees who actively engage in wellness activities appear to be less stressed than employees who do not.

2. Wellness programs can be fun and exciting, especially those which include friendly competition and contests.

3. Incentives like lower health care premiums for active program participants will drive employees to participate in your wellness program.

4. Healthy and happy employees are likely to stay with companies who promote wellness.

5. Healthy employees cost less and tend to be more productive than their unhealthy counterparts.

A few cons:

1. Employees do not like being forced into making life-style changes, even if those changes will benefit them in the long run. No pun intended.

2. Disincentives like increased health care premiums for unhealthy lifestyle choices like smoking, etc. tend to alienate employees. They can come back to bite you in more ways than one.

3. Employees may view your efforts to secure health assessment information as an invasion of their privacy.

Wellness programs come in all sizes and shapes. They range from healthy living newsletters to onsite fitness facilities.

Some examples:

- Providing space for instructors and structured exercise.

- Providing gym memberships or negotiating discounted memberships for employees.

- Wellness bulletin boards.

- Conducting health fairs.

- Establishing employee activities committees.

- Bringing in outside speakers for wellness "lunch and learns."

- Promoting or sponsoring participation in community walks and runs.

- Participating in corporate fitness challenges.

- Offering flu shots.

- Paycheck stuffer wellness tips.

- Conducting weight loss team competitions.

- Offering health risk assessments.

- Dedicating space in vending machines for healthy snacks.

- Offering fresh fruits and healthy snacks in meetings instead of cookies and donuts.

And the list goes on!

The major challenge will be encouraging your employees to change behaviors to improve their wellness and general well-being. You need to realize the best you can do is to offer something, make it fun, lead by example, promote it, recognize successes and then, stay the course. In many cases, the sheer enthusiasm and momentum that builds with your program will be enough encouragement for employees to participate.

Here I Am. Does Anybody See Me?

I have been fairly accused of "only knowing what I know" from time to time so I decided to take a big leap forward. Instead of launching into the importance of employee recognition based on my thoughts and experiences from my many years of working in Human Resources, I decided to go to the all-knowing and all-seeing Internet and conduct a search on employee recognition programs. Am I ever glad I did! I learned about e-cards and e-greetings. I explored several sites where I can purchase everything from beach balls with company logos on them to fancy pen and pencil sets. And, even better, I read the creation of an employee recognition program is a "great way to push workers to excel." Really! Good luck with that!

Let's start this discussion where it should have begun in the first place. Employee recognition is not rocket science. When is the last time you received a personal note of thanks from someone? How did it make you feel? If you are like most people, your world was a bit brighter that day and your load was a bit lighter. It doesn't matter at what level an employee works in an organization. We are all not so different. We all want to feel like we are part of something good and important. We all want to be able to use our skills and talents to make meaningful contributions and we all feel really good about it when those contributions are recognized and appreciated.

So, how do we get there from here? Resist the temptation of developing a fancy flavor of the month employee recognition program and then spending several weeks writing up a detailed and elaborate policy to describe it. I suggest you schedule a one-hour brainstorming session with your supervisors and managers, talk through their ideas and recommendations on the kinds of performance and achievements that warrant recognition in your business, agree on some different forms the recognition can take, empower them to begin recognizing their employees and set them free to do so. Remember, it is not the monetary value of the recognition that matters. It is the sincerity with which it is given and the message it sends.

Performance Appraisal -
Who Says It Has To Be Complicated?

First things first. Before I get into the "how" of performance appraisal, let's spend some time talking about the "why." If you don't have a good answer to why you are doing performance appraisal you should probably stop doing it and spend your time elsewhere because you will not be getting maximum value from your process.

There are several good reasons why you should be conducting performance appraisals.

1. Most employees really do want to know how they are doing.

2. Performance appraisal discussions provide a wonderful opportunity for two-way communication between supervisors and employees.

3. Performance appraisal ratings provide meaningful input to management for future compensation and promotion decisions.

4. Performance appraisal discussions pave the way for employee development.

5. Performance appraisals may actually result in improved employee productivity.

6. Performance appraisal results may provide legal defensibility for future termination actions.

As to the "how" of performance appraisal, I have been guilty on many occasions of over-thinking the process and getting more hung up on what the forms look like than on providing clear guidelines for supervisors and employees on how to have a meaningful discussion and on what they should be striving to accomplish. Maybe this sounds familiar to you, too. If ever there was a place to employ the KISS theory, "keep it simple, stupid," this is the place.

The following are recommended considerations for you as

you design or redesign an employee performance appraisal process:

1. Performance appraisal with professional and salaried employees can be as simple as a supervisor and a subordinate sitting down with a blank sheet of paper. I really do mean a blank sheet of paper. The objective of their meeting is to leave the discussion in agreement on 3-5 key areas the employee should focus on during the appraisal period. The supervisor has veto power and final say on what those 3-5 areas are. Then, a couple of times throughout the year, they should sit down and discuss progress toward the agreed upon objectives. At the end of the performance period, they sit down one more time and the supervisor appraises the employee's full year of performance. It really is as simple as that.

2. Performance appraisal for hourly paid employees, if they perform more specific and/or routine work, should be more prescriptive. If their work is neither specific nor routine, see above. If it is, I suggest selecting and appraising them on 5-6 areas within their control such as quality, safety, reliability, housekeeping, job knowledge and productivity.

3. Ten performance ratings are too many. I swear I have seen performance appraisal systems with ten ratings. Three ratings are probably too few. You might like the word "outstanding" more than you do "excellent" or prefer the word "unsatisfactory" to "unacceptable." It doesn't really matter. What does matter is that you choose an agreed upon number of ratings, define them to the best of your ability and then agree as a management team that you will do your absolute best to

live by them. I cannot begin to count the number of times when push came to shove and it was time to select employees for a layoff that one manager after another would line up at my door to tell me why their employee, previously rated "satisfactory", really wasn't. I understand every manager and every supervisor wants to have a positive and upbeat performance appraisal discussion with each or their employees. That's OK if your organization is willing to live with those inflated ratings.

4. If I designed a new performance appraisal process today, I would have four ratings. They would be outstanding, satisfactory, needs improvement and unsatisfactory. That's just me.

5. I like self-appraisals. They give employees an active role in the process and some ownership as well. Also, many managers and supervisors are responsible for many employees, and while it would be great if they could remember every significant achievement or failure of each of their subordinates, they don't. Yes, self-appraisals may become a crutch for some managers but, in my experience, this is the exception and not the rule. Another thing self-appraisals can do for you is to help managers and subordinates get back on the same page. I recall receiving a beautifully written list of accomplishments from a subordinate that had very little to do with the objectives we had agreed upon at the beginning of the year. It turns out this particular employee was very good at doing the things he wanted to do though they had very little to do with what he was being paid to do.

Remember, this whole performance appraisal business will only be as complicated as you allow it to be.

Organization Reviews Are Not Just For The Big Dogs

So tell me, which organization would you rather work for, the New York Yankees or the St. Louis Cardinals? All baseball allegiances aside, though I freely admit to being a diehard Cardinals fan, I would choose the St. Louis Cardinals' organization every time. I want to be part of an organization with a good farm system and a strong preference for hiring from within. I think most employees would agree with me.

Organization review time, you might call it talent review or succession planning time, was always my favorite time of the year. I came alive. I loved the preparation and the time spent talking with key managers about their employees, themselves and their organization issues, challenges and opportunities.

I learned some useful lessons along the way about successful organization review processes and the development of good farm systems.

1. All employees should be considered in your process, not just the big dogs.

2. All employees should be given the opportunity to tell you what their career aspirations are as part of your organization review process preparation.

3. There are as many organization review forms and templates out there as there are companies. Prepare your leadership team with whatever information it takes for them to have a meaningful discussion on the

performance, potential and readiness to do more for the employees they intend to discuss.

4. The following should be candidly discussed and clearly identified in your organization review meeting:

- The strengths and weaknesses of all talent in your organization.

- Identification of those employees in your organization with the greatest potential to do more.

- Successors and their readiness to step into key positions.

- Non-performers and the development of action plans for improvement or removal.

- Skills gaps for key positions.

- Plans for communicating back to the employees what was discussed about them during your review.

As Human Resources leaders, these may be the most important meetings we facilitate each year.

Do We Do What We Say We Do?

Many years ago, I had the privilege of leading the Human Resources function for a large group of manufacturing companies. I felt strongly about our responsibility to employees to do the things we told them we would do to support them. While we worked very hard at being clear with our practices, policies and procedures for employees, and at being clear in our expectations of our HR staff in the field, I never felt totally confident the right hand knew what the left hand was doing. This became evident when, in a period of less than a couple of weeks, two things happened to us. The first had to do with a workplace violence incident at one of our manufacturing facilities that could have been easily handled had the site HR Manager communicated and posted the new workplace violence policy that had been sent to him months earlier. Upon further investigation, we found it sitting in the bottom of his in-basket. Yes, we really had those things a long time ago. I no longer recall the second incident but the point is it should not have occurred.

We failed our employees in both of those situations and we did not hold up our end of the deal by "doing what we say we do." These failures became the impetus for reflection and then, action. What started out as a very simple exercise of seeking answers to the question, "Do we do what we say we do?" resulted in the creation of a very effective Human Resources self-appraisal tool.

This requires a bit of explanation. At the time, I was working with a very senior and seasoned HR professional. We basically had joint responsibility for multiple sites and thousands of manufacturing employees. On the day in question, it was decided we would split our areas of responsibility: communications, employee relations, performance appraisal, training, policies and procedures, employee opinion survey follow-up, affirmative action, safety, environmental, workers' compensation, security, ethics, budget, HRIS, hiring practices, employee retention, compensation, benefits and recognition. We independently developed questions for each of the subject areas that required nothing more than a simple yes or no response to the primary question at hand. I repeat, "Do we do what we say we do?" The result was 16 pages of questions. We created our self-appraisal tool in the early 90s. I am still using it today, though tweaked and updated many times.

How did we apply it? We sent the self-appraisal template out to each of our facility HR Managers. We asked them to complete it with their staff. Once completed, we scheduled onsite review meetings to talk through their responses. As you might imagine, we didn't have any facility answer "yes" on all of the questions, but that really wasn't our goal. Our goal was to ensure we were doing for employees what we said we would do to support them, and where we weren't, to get back on track.

If we in HR are to be true employee advocates we should enjoy facilitating the activities mentioned above like safety, wellness, employee recognition and performance management. Doing what we say we will do will come easily to us. If we make these things happen in our organizations we are putting our money where our mouth is and we are not only telling our employees what we will do for them, we are proving it.

4

Ethics

Business Ethics - Your Employees Are Watching You!
HR practitioners should be comfortable being the eyes and ears and conscience of the organization. I have always felt this was an appropriate expectation and relished the responsibility because nothing is more important than the manner in which a company conducts its business. I don't know about you but I refuse to support unethical businesses. I will take my business elsewhere. The same goes for where I choose to work.

What about our employees? We earn our reputation with our employees every day through the things we do and the things we say inside and outside of our place of employment. We want our employees to trust us. In order to earn their trust, they need to see us doing the right thing and leading by example. They need to be encouraged to make good choices and to feel free to come to us when they have failed to do so or when they see others making bad choices. They have to be able to do so without fear of retaliation.

The menu for success is a pretty simple one.

1. Tell employees what you expect.

2. Give them lots of good examples of acceptable and un-acceptable behaviors.

3. Lead by example. Your employees really are watching you!

4. Take decisive action when unacceptable behavior is brought to your attention and validated.

5. Remind employees of your expectations on a regular basis.

6. Do not allow any employee to be retaliated against for speaking up and doing the right thing.

5

Communications

Effective Communications - Really!

I love talking about communications! One size does not fit all but I have found that companies who do it best seem to have a lot in common. They all work hard to encourage and promote two-way communication. They understand and appreciate that their employees want to know what is going on in the business and want to be asked for their input on how to make improvements. They openly discuss business plans and strategies, they reduce their communications plan to writing for all to see and they give someone, usually Human Resources, the responsibility for monitoring the effectiveness of their efforts.

So, what about us mere mortals? How do we go about improving our communications? The conundrum is that no company communicates enough. Employees will always tell you that they want more communications but companies cannot be expected to spend all of their time communicating. It's the real world and companies have to deal with it. On a daily basis, they will be faced with the need to communicate, the desire to meet employee expectations for communications while, at the same time, profitably producing or providing a product or service.

I think an appropriate starting point for companies of any size is to take a complete inventory of all forms of communication within their operation. Even companies who may feel their efforts are lacking will be surprised by the amount of time they spend communicating. If a commitment to communicate is already present, companies may need to examine the form their communications take and the effectiveness of their delivery. I was always saddened and disappointed when I asked a management team to tell me about their communications plan or strategy and they would puff out their chests and start waxing eloquently about their internal website, company newsletter or electronic messaging boards. Don't get me wrong, these are all perfectly acceptable methods of communication but they lack two very key ingredients of effective communication. They are neither face-to-face nor do they allow for two-way exchange.

I believe companies should concentrate their time and effort on providing as much "live" communication as possible. I would suggest there are five key building blocks that constitute the foundation of an effective communications program. Anything beyond these five is icing on the cake.

They are:
1. An annual state-of-the-business address.

2. Monthly site meetings.

3. Weekly staff and supervisor meetings.

4. Weekly toolbox meetings.

5. An employee opinion survey every 1-2 years.

Annual State-of-the-Business Address
- The meeting should be 45 minutes to 1 hour in length.

- The audience includes all employees.

- The meeting should be conducted by the business leader. This meeting should never be delegated downward

- The meeting is designed for communicating the current business situation, strategic goals and business objectives. Typical agenda items include an economic climate update, financial results, customer feedback, future strategies, employee recognition and employees' role in achieving future goals and objectives

- This meeting is an opportunity to engage employees and encourage them to ask questions though very few will actually take you up on it in such a setting.

- Know your audience, resist the temptation to wow them with fancy technical and financial jargon and keep the PowerPoint slides simple and to a minimum.

Monthly Site Meetings
- The meeting should be conducted by the top management individual at the location.

- The audience is a randomly selected group of 10-12 employees.

- Lunchtime meetings are ideal.

- The primary objectives of this meeting are to establish relationships and build rapport with your employees and to stay close to the pulse of what is going on in your workplace

- The meeting is focused less on a business agenda and more on getting to know the people in the room.

- This meeting can also be used to dispel rumors and to give face-to-face recognition for special achievements by anyone in the room.

Weekly Staff And Supervisor Meetings

- These are two separate and distinct meetings.

- Each meeting should be 45 minutes to 1 hour in length.

- The audience is facility staff (department heads) and facility supervisors.

- The focus of these meetings is on the achievement of business and department goals for facility staff members and production goals for the supervisors of hourly paid employees.

- These meetings are an opportunity to celebrate successes and to discuss areas such as employee turnover, employee relations issues, policy and procedures updates and location rumors.

Weekly Toolbox Meetings

- These are 10-15 minute stand-up meetings conducted with shop floor employees in their actual work area.

- This meeting is an opportunity for supervisors to

cascade much of the information they received in their weekly supervisor meeting, i.e. production schedule performance and highlights, safety and housekeeping, quality, policy and procedures updates, etc.

- This meeting is a wonderful forum for giving recognition to employees in front of their co-workers.

Employee Opinion Survey

- The audience is all employees.

- While the employee opinion survey administration meeting itself is one-way by nature, the later meetings and discussion of survey results are an excellent opportunity for two-way communication.

There are many ways in which a company can improve the effectiveness of their communications with employees. The five methods I have described above are in no way intended to be presented as the only approach to effective communications. They are simply methods I have seen work time and time again.

Employee Opinion Surveys: The Granddaddy Of Them All!

I am an employee opinion survey nerd. I love working with them. I love talking about them. I recently facilitated the development, execution, action planning and communication of an employee opinion survey for a good friend of mine who owns several restaurants. I had as much fun working through the process with him and his senior staff as I did when I started working with employee opinion surveys in 1981. There is no better way to show employees you really care about them than to ask them how they feel about their work and their workplace and then to act on what they tell you.

Throughout my entire working career, I never encountered a better platform for communications than the employee opinion survey. Furthermore, I never encountered a better company than the Emerson Electric Co. on how to get the most out of one. The reason I mention Emerson is not because they have developed the best set of questions. Anyone can develop a good employee opinion survey questionnaire. It's because employee opinion surveys have been the cornerstone of their communications and employee relations efforts worldwide since 1959. Their commitment to the process is incredible.

Developing and conducting an employee opinion survey is actually a very simple process.

1. *Questionnaire development* - Fewer questions are better than more. Somewhere between 40 and 50 is probably best. If you go much higher you begin to repeat yourself.

2. *Narrative question development* - Employee opinion surveys should allow employees the option to provide written comments on all survey questions. I also like to give employees the opportunity to respond to two seemingly simple questions: "What do you like most about working here?" and "What do you like least about working here?"

3. *Work group determination* - To protect the anonymity of employees, each of your work groups should consist of at least 10 employees. Work groups should be

specific so issues can be pinpointed for attention and resolution.

4. *Opinion survey administration script development* - You will want to develop a written script to ensure all employees in your organization receive a consistent message on what you are trying to accomplish by conducting your survey.

5. *Survey administration* - Opinion surveys can be administered online or by employees sitting down in a room with paper forms and pencils. It doesn't matter. Do it whichever way is most efficient for you.

6. *Presentation of the survey results* - Opinion survey results can be presented in a number of ways. At a minimum, you will want to compile and analyze overall results and individual work group results.

7. *Survey analysis* - While the numbers and written comments will tell you a story and give you a pulse of employee feelings by work group, contextual information received from employee feedback sessions is crucial to understanding your findings.

8. *Communication of results* – This critical step is where the real work begins and is generally the most time-consuming and expensive part of the process. This is where you get to validate what you think the survey results are telling you and to probe for clarification of issues. If you are not willing to commit to an open sharing and discussion of the results with your employees in a non-defensive manner, do not ask your employees to complete a survey in the first place. If you ask your employees to tell you what they really think about their

workplace and then fail to act on what they tell you, you will have missed a wonderful opportunity for two-way communications and, instead, inadvertently created an employee relations disaster.

9. *Action planning* – After the results have been analyzed and shared with employees, it is time to develop a written action plan to address employee concerns. The final action plan should be shared with employees and progress toward completion of action items should be communicated on a regular basis.

Your Employees Are Talking To You. Are You Listening?

As previously stated, I recently facilitated an employee opinion survey for a very proactive and progressive business-owner friend of mine in the fast food industry. As part of his survey, we asked his employees two questions that required a written response. (1) What do you like most about working here? (2) What do you like least about working here?

He gave me permission to share a sample of the actual written responses we received to each of the questions. I should note that over 700 employees from multiple restaurants had the opportunity to submit written comments. My reason for sharing his employees' comments is to provide a glimpse of what is on the minds of many employees today regarding their work and their workplace. I have been working with employee opinion surveys and the written comments that go along with them for over 35 years. These comments are neither unique nor industry-specific. It is very likely your employees would respond in a similar fashion if given the opportunity. The question is whether or not you know which of your employees feel which way and in which part of the organization they are working so you can address those issues and concerns.

What They Liked Most:

- "Our management team is fair and fun but also assertive. For the most part, we get the shifts and the hours we want. If we have a problem, our management addresses it accordingly. We are treated with respect. Our store is a great place to work. I recommend it to all of my friends."

- "The staff and management are all friendly and welcomed me when I first started. I make decent money. I enjoy being able to let my personality shine at work. Managers are nice and are here to help out. I like the opportunity I have for job growth here."

- "I love our management team. We have wonderful staff members for the most part. We all seem to work great together. I always feel at home with my job. I can be having a terrible day and come to work my shift and instantly feel better. I have a wonderful time at work and love being here."

- "I like that everyone is accepted here no matter who you are as a person."

- "I like that I am frequently told that I am doing a good job and I am often used as an example to encourage other workers."

- "I appreciate that my manager is considerate of my life outside of work."

- "I like how everyone has a positive attitude and are quick to help someone out if they are struggling. It is a clean and respectful work environment."

- "If I have a problem my management team listens and is always willing to help me with it."

- "I like the flexibility of the hours and the diverse group of people I work with."

- "I like that I am surrounded by good people at work every day."

What They Liked Least:

- "Management does not lead by example. Favoritism is super bad between my managers and co-workers."

- "I don't like it when higher-ups come in and there is no eye contact or communication."

- "I understand that criticism is needed sometimes and I gladly accept it but not when it is carried out in an unprofessional manner. I also feel I can never speak up if I think something should change."

- "Evaluations for raises are random and loosely based on performance."

- "As an employee, I should not have to apologize to customers about the way my General Manager speaks to me in front of them."

- "Some managers have a tendency to talk down to me just because they are higher up. Don't talk to me like I am a child. Talk to me with respect. Also, on most days, management walks around and does nothing. If that is all it takes to be in management, sign me up. If you want respect, you give respect."

- "I dislike hearing about all of the drama in other peoples' lives and all of the talking about people behind their backs."

- "Policies are enforced differently depending on who they are applied to."

- "Disagreements in my store are not handled appropriately and are rarely resolved."

- "I dislike people who get away with things because they are more liked than others."

My friend is listening to and addressing what his employees are talking about. Are you?

6

Employee Engagement

Why Are We Still Talking About Employee Engagement?
I am a pack rat. When I come across an interesting statistic, practice or article I like, I file it away. Admittedly, it is a rather crude filing system. What I really do is just throw it in my desk drawer. I recently came across a single sheet of paper from a presentation I had given many years ago. It contained some compelling statistics from an article on Super Motivation written by a Mr. Dean R. Spritzer, AMACON, 1995.

The statistics:

- 73% of employees say they are less motivated today than they used to be.

- 84% of employees say they could perform significantly better if they wanted to.

- 50% of employees say they are only putting in enough effort into their work to hold onto their jobs.

Yikes! Those are some scary statistics. While I understand the age of the data may be troublesome to some, I have to believe the numbers are still very much true, or are at least directionally correct based on all I have read and heard in recent years. I also believe you need baseline information or some way of sizing a problem you are facing before you can put plans in action to solve it.

What can a company do to assess their level of employee engagement? I have mentioned before how strongly I feel about the power and value of employee opinion surveys. While an employee opinion survey would certainly be helpful in gauging the level of employee engagement in your business, the typical surveys I am familiar with are too general in scope. Back to my desk drawer filing system. Yep, I found an answer in the form of an employee engagement survey from the Gallup Management Journal by Thackray, J. 2001, March 15, entitled "Feedback for Real?"

His survey questionnaire consisted of the following eleven employee engagement questions:

1. Do you know what is expected of you at work?

2. Do you have the materials and equipment you need to perform your job well?

3. At work, do you have the opportunity to do what you do best every day?

4. In the last 7 days, have you received recognition or praise for doing good work?

5. Does your supervisor, or someone at work, seem to care about you as a person?

6. Is there someone at work who encourages your development?

7. At work, do your opinions seem to count?

8. Does the mission/purpose of your company make you feel your job is important?

9. Are your fellow employees committed to doing quality work

10. In the last 6 months, has someone at work talked to you about your progress?

11. In the past year, have you had opportunities to learn and grow?

I asked my HR staff to respond to these questions a few years ago. The results were enlightening and useful. I have also in-corporated many of the questions above into recent employee opinion survey questionnaires I have developed.

7

Technology, Tools, Goals and Analytics

I asked a friend and former peer of mine to review a draft of my book. He commented, "I like your approach of going back to the basics but at the same time I think it is important to maximize the technology and tools available in this modern world. Even a caveman has to "tweet" every once in a while. I love the hands on, floor time and face-to-face approaches but advise your readers to use the latest technologies like HR portal, Facebook and LinkedIn to make them more efficient." I couldn't have said it better myself.

What's In Your Toolbox?

Imagine this. You receive a call. You are being hired as the head of Human Resources for the ABC Company. The ABC Company has been in business for many years. They have several domestic and international locations. It will be your responsibility to shape and then lead the Human Resources function for the company. While at the outset this may seem like a daunting task, it is actually quite simple. This is the time for you to call upon your education, your experiences and all of your resources and tools from the past. The first thing you will need is data, all kinds of data. What is the reputation on the HR function at the ABC Company? Is the right HR staff in place to support the organization? Does the HR staff spend their time working on the right things? Does the HR staff know how employees feel about the company and about their workplace? And, the list of questions goes on.

I have had the opportunity to answer many of these same questions in the past. In each of these situations, I reached into my toolbox and worked with these five "tried and true" basic tools.

1. Employee Opinion Surveys - I will continue to say, until I am blue in the face, there is no better way to get the pulse of your workforce and a baseline of feelings about an organization than through a properly administered and well-executed employee opinion survey.

2. HR Self-Appraisal - As previously discussed, a comprehensive Human Resources self-appraisal is a cumbersome and tedious tactical exercise but it is a fantastic way to determine the extent to which your HR function is supporting your company and your employees.

3. HR Function Process Mapping - The objective of this tactical exercise is to determine exactly how and on what projects and tasks your HR staff is spending their time. As I will discuss later in Chapter Eight, the outcome of process mapping your HR function will

always be eye opening and should always result is some shifting of priorities.

4. HR Reviews - A comprehensive Human Resources Review is a wonderful strategic exercise in which, on an annual basis, HR leadership and senior management spend an entire day discussing the HR agenda and expected HR deliverables for the company. Everything HR leads, impacts or touches is examined. Topics include communications, compensation, supervision, recruiting, training and development, succession planning, ethics, safety, wellness, employee activities, community involvement, practices, policies and procedures. Like the outcome of HR function process mapping, this exercise will generally result in a list of action items, a clarification of priorities and HR and senior leadership getting on the same page.

5. HR Function SWOT Analysis - I have always been able to gain tremendous insight and perspective into the HR function of a company by conducting a strengths, weaknesses, opportunities and threats (SWOT) analysis. Soon after joining a new company, I would immediately conduct a SWOT with the HR staff and then with a group of senior managers. Understanding early on what your HR staff and senior managers feel about these four areas is a great springboard for getting started and quickly coming up to speed in a new assignment.

It is easy to get side-tracked with the issues of the day in a new assignment. Fight the urge and make time to use the tools that helped you get the new role in the first place. My five tools served me well throughout my career. What's in your toolbox?

The Data Will Set You Free!

I have a close friend and former co-worker who lived by this mantra. He was a data miner. It is hard and tedious work but he was a true believer in the value of going inside the data, inside the numbers, to find answers and to solve problems. His approach made me curious. What would I find if I went inside my HR data, my HR numbers? The result was a major process-mapping project with the goal of determining exactly how my HR staff was spending their time (me, too) and the amount of time we were spending by activity. We process mapped everything - employee relations, staffing, employee health and safety, compensation and benefits, organization planning and development, business partnering, communications, training, special projects, compliance, HR strategy and community relations.

My friend was right. The data did set us free. It told us we were very good at blocking and tackling and handling day-to-day issues but were spending way too much time on administrative activities and way too little time on communications, employee development and proactive and positive employee relations.

I have initiated comprehensive process mapping exercises twice in my career. Both times, it was a long and tedious process. Both times, the results were an eye opener that resulted in some realignment of responsibilities and priorities for the function. It worked for me. I wonder what it would tell you.

HR Goal Setting. Getting Started.

Every year around mid-October, the subject of calendar year goal setting comes up. Maybe you are responsible for writing HR goals for your organization for the first time. Maybe you are doing it for the 25th time. It doesn't really matter. In either situation, the starting point will always be the same blank sheet of paper.

Since 1981, when the acronym was first introduced, we have all been encouraged to write S.M.A.R.T. goals. We know our goals should be Specific, Measurable, Achievable, Relevant and Time-based. It was good advice in 1981 and it is still good advice today so we should all plan on writing S.M.A.R.T. goals again for next year.

As you contemplate what those S.M.A.R.T. goals should be for HR in the coming year, it never hurts to do a little bit of research to see what your fellow HR colleagues are planning.

I decided to conduct an Internet search on HR goal setting. I came across the following curious goal, "Human Resources will contribute to Company X's mission and vision by living our vision of providing a seamless, consistent, customer-focused and quality-driven system of services, products, tools and programs to ensure a competent, vibrant and diverse workforce." What? Really! So much for what at least one organization is in for from their HR function next year.

Let's get back to the basics, which means keeping things simple and keeping things clear. After going through the annual ritual of setting HR goals for over 30 years, and after having spent an inordinate amount of time trying to be fresh and creative from year to year, I have come to the realization that my HR goal setting has always boiled down to the same two goal areas. I always set goals around "employee development and retention" and "improving employee satisfaction."

Start with these two goal areas the next time you sit down with your blank sheet of paper. Tailor your goals to what is happening in and around your organization and you will do just fine supporting your business and your employees.

8

Practices, Policies, and Procedures

This was a difficult chapter to write. There are so many practices, policies and procedures to choose from. I decided to focus on areas that were the most impactful to me and the organizations I worked in if I "didn't" get them right.

Who Gets To Stay?

I hate layoffs. However, I live in a real world and I understand there are times when they become a necessity. I have seen many companies try to wish and hope their way through down markets and dark days. This is a flawed strategy. I have seen companies avoid layoffs through the use of short work weeks and furloughs. These strategies do work but cease to be effective when conditions stay tough through prolonged periods of time.

I would suggest there are three key steps a company can take in order to be prepared for a layoff.

1. Determine layoff criterion that suits your business needs.

2. Commit your layoff policy to writing.

3. Communicate the policy to all employees.

This is not as easy as it sounds. There are several criteria to consider when deciding who has to go and who gets to stay. Some examples are skills and abilities, seniority, performance appraisal of record, disciplinary action and potential. I have always favored using skills and abilities and performance appraisal of record with seniority as a tie breaker. You should pick what will work best for you in your business. What does matter is that you reduce your choices to writing and you clearly communicate your layoff policy to all employees. Layoffs are horrible things. Don't make things worse by leading employees to believe you are randomly picking and choosing who is to be affected.

Hire Slowly, Fire Quickly

There are a lot of versions of this theme that have been written through the years. That is a step in the right direction because it is an important subject. Here is my version.

I know. I know. It is maddening for Human Resources professionals when everyone is calling and screaming at you about their open requisitions and how they absolutely must have them filled immediately or the company as you know it will cease to exist. It happens all of the time. It always has, it always will. The company gets a big order. The "season" is right around the corner. The need for a number of new employees is great and the need for them is now. While I understand and appreciate the need for speed, I also understand what can happen to an organization that goes after warm bodies or, as I have actually heard it so eloquently stated, "anyone who can fog the glass."

I would suggest the impact of hiring the wrong employee is far more damaging to your business than the impact of taking the necessary amount of time required to source the right employee. To illustrate my point, I recommend you calculate the true cost of turnover in your organization. Include every cost in your process from start to finish. The direct costs include all time and money spent on advertising, recruitment, selection, training and even the time associated with exit interviews of those who choose to leave you. You will be shocked. Next, consider the message you are sending to employees when they are expected to work alongside someone who is clearly not suited for employment. So, slow down and take a breath. Become more efficient with your hiring process but take the time it takes to get it right. In the end, you will have a much more productive workforce and much lower turnover costs.

Fire quickly! This is a simple concept. Let me explain. I am saying "quickly", not capriciously or without considerable thought to ensure your decision is the correct one. Telling someone, "You don't get to work here anymore" is the toughest thing HR professionals ever do. If this doesn't make you feel sick to your stomach leading up to it and after it, it's probably time for you to find another line of work. But, once the decision has been made, suck it up and get on with it. It does not get any easier with time. Do what is best for the organization, do it in a respectful way, and move on.

Employee Retention - Keeping The Good Ones

I have worked in and with companies and industries with little to no employee turnover. I have worked with and in industries where 150% annual turnover was common. The one characteristic all of these companies had in common is that none of them took their employee retention levels for granted. They all worked hard at doing whatever they could to keep their good employees.

Call them retention strategies or call them attributes of low turnover companies. It doesn't matter. What does matter is that a commitment to selecting and then executing some of the items below from my "senior management retention to-do checklist" will result in lower turnover.

Senior Management Retention Checklist

1. Train your interviewers to ensure they can clearly articulate your plans and your culture. Getting the right people through the door in the first place will increase your chances of being able to retain them.

2. Follow up frequently with new employees during their first 180 days. Yes, I said 180 days. Actually create a list of the specific areas you wish to cover with them. The focus should be on the new employee and on how they feel about their new job.

3. Provide "on-the-job buddies" for new employees to help them learn the ropes. It's good for the new employee and it is recognition and development for the mentor.

4. Randomly select and ask employees what keeps them at your company. Asking has positive side effects. You

will uncover general areas of concern that need to be addressed. The employees you speak with will feel cared about and valued. Simply asking the question is a retention strategy.

5. Do your absolute best to ensure your pay and benefits are competitive with like companies in the area.

6. Employee retention is not a Human Resources program. It is a management process and everyone needs to be actively involved. Assemble a multi-disciplined group of managers, supervisors and employees to help you analyze reasons for your turnover and develop action plans for reducing it. Spread the ownership for employee retention at your company.

7. Create a culture and workplace that prides itself in showing visible respect for employees as being responsible and achieving adults.

8. Develop policies and procedures that support rather than prohibit or intimidate your employees. What is the "tone" of your employee policies and procedures?

9. Develop a formal communications plan, communicate it to your employees and stick to it.

10. Actively participate in your new employee orientation process. Imagine how you would feel if you are the new employee sitting in orientation and the CEO, Plant Manager or senior most person in the business pops their head in and personally welcomes you to the company and tells you they are glad you have joined the company. It matters!

11. Model the culture you promote in your workplace. Lead by example

12. Be visible in the workplace and take the time to notice your employees. Don't become too busy and focused on the mission at hand to pay attention to the little things like saying "good morning" or "thanks" or asking an employee how things are going and really listening to their answer.

13. I, and a whole lot of other people, contend the number one reason employees leave companies is to get away from bad managers or bad supervisors. Please understand the one behavior employees will not tolerate for long is disrespect.

14. Develop a process for identifying ineffective supervisors and managers. Then, work with them or part ways with them.

15. A workplace that is seen as being caring and fun-loving generates enthusiasm. Don't take yourself too seriously.

16. Pictures, pictures, pictures! Take them, post them on bulletin boards and then give them to employees.

17. Encourage employees to take advantage of your open door policy. Take the time to listen to what they have to say when they use it and respond to their questions and issues in a timely manner.

18. Recognize and celebrate company successes.

There are no silver bullets here. No single approach will lower turnover at your company. It is a lot of things and they will differ from company to company. Take some time to assess your workplace and the methods you are currently relying on to retain your employees. If your turnover is low and you feel all of your bases are covered, great. Congratulations! If not, concentrate your efforts on a few of the items from the list above and see what they do for you over time.

Why Do You Stay?

Take a minute and think about how much time and effort you have spent on exit interviews where you work or where you have worked in the past. Now, ask yourself, "Did our retention levels change as a result of these efforts? Did we ever really do anything with all of those completed exit interview forms?" If you are like most HR practitioners I know and if you work in a company like most of the companies I have worked in or am familiar with, very little changed as a result of your exit interview process. Trust me. I know it has nothing to do with the amount of effort you put into it.

I've seen the exit interview questionnaires. I've written the questionnaires. They all go something like this:

1. What was your primary reason for leaving?
2. What did you like most about your job?
3. What did you like least about your job?
4. Tell us about your immediate supervisor.
5. Did you have the necessary tools, materials and support to do your job?
6. Was your job performance evaluated fairly?
7. Would you consider working here again at some time in the future?
8. Is there anything we can do to encourage you to stay?

9. Do you have any recommendations for making our company a better place to work?

The list of questions can go on and on. For the most part, the questions above are all good ones. The problem here is you are asking them to the wrong people and at the wrong time. In reality, the exiting employee doesn't really care about helping you out so life will be better at the company he or she has decided to leave. This view is understandable. If you were so concerned about them as an employee you should have been asking them all of these same questions while they were still working for you. Your exiting employee is correct. All of those questions could have been asked during performance appraisal, your organization review process or even when you conducted an employee opinion survey.

I am not recommending you quit conducting exit interviews but I would suggest you supplement your process with one additional step that worked very well for me throughout my career. I always found it to be far more valuable and enlightening to seek out long-service employees and ask them, "Why do you stay?" rather than tracking down leavers to ask them, "Why are you leaving?"

Temporary Employees - The Good, The Bad, The Ugly!
Good, bad and ugly may not be the best descriptors of temporary employees but, hopefully, you get my point. There are many pros and cons to consider before deciding if the utilization of temporary employees is right for you. The fact remains that more and more companies are relying on temporary employees to supplement their workforce than ever before. An

article I read in 2013 claimed temporary employee hiring was up 50% since the recession ended 5 years ago. The same article put the number of temporary employees in the U.S. at roughly 2.7 million with 1/3 of them working in manufacturing. I only mention 1/3 of them working in manufacturing to dispel the myth that temporary employees *only* work in manufacturing. The takeaway here is an obvious one. The widespread use of temporary employees is here to stay and you may be missing the competitiveness boat if you do not get on board.

While the use of temporary employees is not a cure-all, it clearly makes sense for some companies. The use of temporary employees makes great sense for companies who need to cover seasonal spikes as well as for companies who are going through periods of market volatility and instability and want to protect their core employees.

Once the decision has been made to supplement your work-force with temporary employees your next decision is whether to "go it alone" or work with a staffing partner. Finding a staffing partner should not be a difficult thing to do. Finding the right staffing partner can be another thing altogether but can be achieved if you do your homework. Having hired temporary employees internally and with staffing partners many times throughout my career, I prefer working with a staffing partner rather than managing the process internally.

In order for the utilization of temporary employees to be a win-win-win proposition we need to take a close look at the pros and cons and answer the question, "What's in it for me?" for each of the interested parties: the employer, the temporary worker and the staffing partner.

Employer Pros And Cons

Pros:

1. Utilizing temporary employees and filling permanent positions from a "temp to perm feeder group" can be a very cost effective hiring and retention strategy.
2. The use of temporary employees affords the employer a sneak peek of employees without having to make an employment commitment.
3. A good staffing partner will ensure the employer always has a pre-qualified pool of candidates at their fingertips.
4. The employer will realize a significant reduction of administrative burden because the staffing partner has responsibility for payroll, tax deductions, workers' compensation, fringe benefits and virtually all paperwork associated with employment applications, payroll information, health insurance enrollment, workers' compensation, terminations and unemployment insurance.
5. The employer will save considerable time and expense because their need to be involved in advertising, recruiting, screening, interviewing and background checking is virtually eliminated.
6. The use of temporary employees provides flexibility and enables businesses to ramp up or down quickly while protecting their core employment base.

Cons:

1. Employers cannot reasonably expect temporary employees to demonstrate the same level of commitment, company loyalty and dedication as their regular employees.

2. Employers may find themselves in a perpetual state of training and new employee orientation.

3. Employers must be prepared to deal with the inherent morale issues that arise when employees work side-by-side and are paid and treated differently.

4. Temporary employees typically have higher turnover rates and a higher incidence of safety issues than most employers experience with their regular workforce.

5. The actual, fully loaded cost of using temporary employees may be higher than the cost of regular staff. You need to do your due diligence here but know that a staffing agency fee structure around 35% is not unusual.

6. Co-employment concerns. This is not necessarily a con but is an area that needs to be understood and managed. To be on the safe side, the American Staffing Association recommends assigning the following responsibilities to your staffing partner:

   - Recruiting

   - Screening

   - Testing

   - Training

   - Interviewing

   - Hiring and firing

   - Assigning and reassigning

   - Handling workers' compensation issues

   - Discipline

   - Distributing paychecks

The A.S.A. also recommends employers establish a "convert or release" policy at 12 months to avoid co-employment ramifications of temporary employees entering into never-ending engagements. The point of these recommendations as well as others around who provides rewards like holiday gifts or performance bonuses is to ensure temporary employees are clear that their employer is your staffing partner and not you

Temporary Employee Pros And Cons

While there are fewer pros and cons for the temporary employee, they are significant and it quickly becomes clear that employment as a temporary employee is not for everyone. The pros are flexibility for the individual, the opportunity to easily move from company to company to find one that suits their needs without entering into an employment commitment, and, for many, the prospect of securing a permanent position with a company if they do a good job. On the downside, in my experience, even in companies who claim to have a hiring model of "temp to perm", very few temporary employees generally end up in permanent assignments. Other cons are the lack of job security, the lack of a clear career path and having an employment status of always being an outsider looking in.

Staffing Partner Considerations

I have chosen a different path for discussing the staffing partner. Instead of speculating on what I feel the pros and cons for the staffing partner might be, I reached out to a former staffing partner colleague and asked him to share with me those things his company wished all of their clients world do better that would result in more successful company-staffing partner relationships. His comments follow.

1. Treat us like a staffing *partner*, not like a staffing *vendor*. Contingent labor is not a necessary evil. It is a strategic business decision for organizations of all sizes to procure talent. Help us help you contain and control risk. Allow your staffing representative to have direct interaction with all hiring managers and end-users. Do not withhold information. Provide us with a true sense of the organization's culture and provide timely feedback and follow-up to ensure our success in finding quality candidates for you.

2. Treat the staffing of temporary employees as a responsibility of your entire organization, not just HR. All areas of the organization need to be in sync with the direction, expectations, processes and desired outcomes of procuring talent.

3. Great staffing companies value relationship, ease of use and overall partnership more than they do high margins. Poor client relationships at high margins drain time and recruiting resources, negatively impact our reputation with candidates and only leads to frustration on both ends.

4. Be proactive rather than reactive. While there will always be a reactive component in our relationship, keeping us informed of upcoming projects, major swings in schedule forecasts, and your views of high performers, underperformers and flight risks will help us both.

5. Manage our results but understand we are the recruiting

experts. That is what we do. Give us the order and then let us do our jobs.

6. Retention should be your number one fulfillment strategy. This may sound counterintuitive coming from your staffing partner but it is true. Clients who value the development, success and retention of their temporary employees typically have a great culture, stability and a positive brand. Staffing companies and contract employees want to work with these companies.

I have given you a lot to think about. The following are some takeaways on the use of temporary employees for me:

1. The use of temporary employees can be a very effective strategy for companies of any size.

2. You can "go it alone" but you will probably be more successful and realize more benefits if you have a staffing partner.

3. Interview prospective staffing companies with the same level of due diligence, intensity and fervor as you would with any other critical business partner or vendor.

4. It is the employer's responsibility and obligation to clearly and openly communicate their temporary employee strategy to all employees.

5. The employer and staffing company have a shared responsibility and obligation to clearly communicate to the temporary employee what's in it for them, i.e. expected duration of assignment, compensation increase schedule, likelihood of moving to a permanent position, etc.

6. It is the employer's responsibility to ensure their

staffing partner has a clear understanding of the skill requirements for each position they are recruiting for, the environment the temporary employee will be asked to work in and the company's culture, business needs and expectations.

7. The staffing company should maintain a full-time presence at the worksite if at all possible.

8. It is the employer's responsibility to communicate and agree on recruiting expectations and performance measures with their staffing partner and then get out of their way and let them do their job.

Welcome To Management! Acclimating New Managers
Congratulations, you made it! Your hard work has paid off and now you are being promoted. You are a manager now. Welcome to management! First things first. Call everyone you know and share your good news. You deserve your limited moment of joy. Had enough of that? Good. Now it is time to get down to business and prepare yourself for what comes next.

The next time you arrive at your workplace your co-workers will see you in a different light and they will expect you to act differently. What's a new manager to do? My advice for any new manager is to relax and take a deep breath. Who you are and how you carry yourself is what earned you your promotion in the first place. This doesn't mean you shouldn't be prepared to make some changes in your approach to workplace situations but it does mean that no major transformation is in order.

What about you, the employer? You have responsibilities and

obligations here, too. You should equip your newly promoted manager with whatever training, orientation and other pearls of wisdom you have in order for your new manager to hit the ground running.

Through the years, I had the opportunity to coach and counsel many new managers as well as many of the department heads and function leaders who promoted them. While the wording has changed a bit through time, the following 10 general management maxims have worked well for me through the years. I think they will work for your new manager, too.

NOTE: I have actually gone so far as having these words laminated on small cards for some new managers so they could have them close by at all times.

1. Never bad-mouth anyone in management to one of your employees. Actually, never bad-mouth anyone to or in front of your employees.

2. There are no rules against being friendly or approachable in the workplace but be careful and maintain an arms length between you and your subordinates. They will be watching closely for consistency of treatment and nobody likes favoritism - not even the favorites.

3. Be inclusive. Be a shining example that diversity and inclusiveness are important to you and to your company.

4. Remind yourself at the start of each day to treat your employees the same way you have always wanted to be treated.

5. No public reprimands. Praise in public. Reprimand in private.

6. You don't have to like the people you work with in order to do a good job but it is a heck of a lot more fun when you do.

7. Lead with integrity and always tell the truth. It is a lot easier than trying to keep track of your lies.

8. Be comfortable in your own skin and be yourself, not the person you think someone else wants you to be.

9. Don't take yourself too seriously. Nobody else does.

10. Make the time to interact with your employees during working hours. There will always be time for paperwork later.

Some Thoughts On Leadership

When I first posted the following thoughts on leadership, it was a general posting. For the sake of this book, I would like for you to change the context to "Human Resources leadership." Everything said below still applies.

You would think it would be easy to find a good description of leadership since so much has been written on the topic throughout history. I actually think it makes it more difficult to boil it down into something simple and practical. After trying, I have come to the realization that leadership, much like beauty, is "in the eye of the beholder." Still, it is a subject worth tackling. I am going to address it in two ways. First, I will share some quotations on leadership that have always resonated with me. Second, I'm going to have some fun with the various styles, skills and qualities that are attributed to leaders.

I chose the following four quotes on leadership because, for me, they are all about being inspirational and instilling confidence. I reflected on these many times throughout my career.

> *"Leadership is lifting a person's vision to high sights, the raising of a person's performance to a higher standard, the building of a personality beyond its normal limitations."* - Peter Drucker

> *"A leader is one who knows the way, goes the way, and shows the way."* - John C. Maxwell

> *"If your actions inspire others to dream more, learn more, do more and become more, you are a leader."* - John Quincy Adams

> *"The day soldiers stop bringing you their problems is the day you have stopped leading them. They have either lost confidence that you can help or have concluded you do not care. Either case is a failure of leadership."* - Colin Powell

The second part of this leadership discussion will likely drive you as crazy as it does me. As I researched leadership styles, qualities and skills, I was unable to find anything that was either reasonably succinct or particularly illuminating. I'll spare you from having to look up those three items and provide a sample of what you will find if you do.

Leadership Styles - autocratic, participative, visionary, coaching, democratic, transactional, affiliative, transformational, commanding, charismatic, innovative, facilitative, strategic, etc.

Leadership Qualities - honesty, courage, integrity, humility, creativity, strategic, sense of humor, positive attitude, ability to inspire, ability to delegate, focus, confidence, intuition, cooperation, ambition, commitment, etc.

Leadership Skills - communication, motivation, delegation, positivity, commitment, organization, flexibility, listening, engaging, trustworthiness, creativity, passion, encouraging, bravery, honesty, know your people, etc.

Clear as mud, right? Is anybody noticing that some of the words in each of the categories do not belong and there is no clear separation between a quality and a skill? No problem! Let's get back to keeping things simple and practical. We are all familiar with shopping. It's unavoidable, so let's be shoppers. I suggest we take the leadership styles, qualities and skills listed above and think of them as department store items. Now, select a couple from each list and shop for the kind of Human Resources leader you would like to be, who you would like to work with. I choose charismatic and participative for style, honesty and integrity as key qualities and communication and motivation as key skills. How about you?

Automatic Wage Progression
For a variety of reasons, many companies do not have a formalized pay system or pay philosophy for their hourly paid factory employees. This can leave employees thinking there is a dart-

board somewhere with a bunch of random rates per hour on it, and when or if their name comes up, a dart is tossed. It doesn't have to be this way.

If you are looking for a simple and effective way to deliver compensation to hourly paid factory employees, I recommend the development of an automatic wage progression structure. It is called "automatic" because step increases are awarded automatically along a set timeline unless an employee is performing at an unsatisfactory level at the time his/her step increase is due.

Step increases are incremental wage increases granted along the way as employees move from the minimum of a wage grade to the maximum or top rate. Step increases are typically awarded at 3 month or 6 month intervals with two primary exceptions. In high turnover businesses and in lower skilled positions, step increases may be awarded every 30 days for the first 90 days as a retention strategy. In more mature operations where employees stay longer and frequently reach the maximum or top rate, once the top rate has been reached, step increases may be considered annually much like they are in a salaried merit increase system. The total amount of time it takes to move from the minimum of a wage grade to the maximum of the grade is based on the amount of time it takes for an average employee to become fully proficient in their job responsibilities within the grade.

Wage Grades

So, what is the ideal number of wage grades? In small operations, there can be as few as three; one for low-skilled, medium-skilled and high-skilled positions. In larger and more complex business operations requiring several types and levels of workers, I would recommend no more than five or six wage grades. You might consider a seventh if you have a large number of group leaders. A rule of thumb is to establish as many wage grades as you have like-skilled groupings of positions keeping in mind that fewer wage grades are easier to manage and communicate.

Determining The Market

In order to be competitive, it is important to base your wage grade structure on what is being paid by local area employers with whom you compete for labor. Some companies will be a better match for your type of operation than others. Some areas for consideration when determining a match are proximity to your location, type of business, headcount and union representation. Once you decide who you wish to compare yourself with you will need wage information. Sources of wage information may include local manufacturing associations, HR associations, Chambers of Commerce, Department of Labor occupational compensation surveys and conducting your own local survey. Regardless of the sources you choose, you should do your best to find companies whose jobs closely match yours.

Transparency

What and why you pay your employees what you do is your business but there is no reason for your compensation structure and pay philosophy to be shrouded in secrecy. I recommend communicating your program and philosophy to employees as well as the basis of your structure. All employees have similar expectations. They want to know what their wage rates are based on, how often they will be reviewed or eligible for increases and the rate of increase they can expect if they are doing a good job. I believe these are reasonable expectations.

9

Conclusion

I started my professional career in Human Resources in 1977. I have had the good fortune of living and working through many years of evolution in our discipline. Gone are the days of "health and happiness" and "Personnel" being responsible for carrying the watermelons to the picnics. Today's HR professional is at the center of the action. S/he is coach, counselor, confidant and teacher. If s/he doesn't have a legal background, s/he keeps contact information of a great employment attorney close by.

Ours is not an exact science. To be effective, one must become comfortable "working in the gray." All employees are different and in most situations there will be more than one way to get it right. It is important to have a network of peers to bounce ideas off of. One regret I have is that I did not make more of an effort to establish an HR network outside of the companies I worked in.

I do not apologize for being an HR caveman. My focus on

the basics and the "tried and true" served me well through the years. I am not suggesting you shouldn't stay abreast of all of the changes in our ever-evolving chosen profession but I am highly recommending that you do not lose sight of the basics that got us here in the first place.

I'm hopeful the tools, lists, advice and suggestions contained in this book will serve as a bit of a primer that can be looked at or referenced from time to time. It has been said that audiences remember the last thing they are told. Assuming that is true, I leave you with two thoughts on what it will take for HR to be successful in the years to come. First, ensure more transparency in communications where you work. Second, ensure more "touches" with employees, not less. Good luck!

Acknowledgements

I had the good fortune of working with many wonderful Human Resources professionals throughout my career. They were my mentors, bosses, peers and subordinates. Today, I call many of them my friends. It is with all of them in mind that I was able to write this book.

I would like to give special thanks to the Human Resources brain trust of Rachel Carvell, Sissy Claxton, Dean Kent and Chris Miller for taking the time to review my book and provide honest and candid feedback. They were my Human Resources voice(s) of reason.

Thank you Brian Clark, my Canadian engineering friend, for your questions, insights and perspectives. You challenged me to look at much of my content through a different lens.

A special thank you to my son, Brian, for his editing support and to my wife, Barbara, who takes over and gets things done once the writing is complete.